SOCIO-ECONOMIC BACKWARDNESS
IN WOMEN

SOCIO-ECONOMIC BACKWARDNESS
IN WOMEN

SOCIO-ECONOMIC BACKWARDNESS IN WOMEN

ANINDITA MUKHERJI
AND
NEELAM VERMA

ASHISH PUBLISHING HOUSE
8/81, Punjabi Bagh, New Delhi-110026

Published by
S.B. **Nangia**
for **Ashish Publishing House**
8/81, Punjabi Bagh,
New Delhi-110026
Tel. 500581
     5410924

ISBN 81-7024-096-4

1987

© Authors

THE FACTS STATED, CONCLUSIONS REACHED AND VIEWS
EXPRESSED IN THIS PROJECT REPORT ARE THE
RESPONSIBILITY OF THE COLLEGE

Printed by :
New Prints
WZ-2026, Rani Bagh
DELHI-110034

ACKNOWLEDGEMENTS

I hereby acknowledge with thanks the services rendered by our teachers, students and staffs of this college in different phases of the study.

I am very much thankful to Dr. (Mrs) Neelam Verma, Lecturer in Psychology of this college for the preparation of interview schedule. She has also taken full responsibility of data analysis and the writing of the project report. But for her cooperation, this project in the present form would not have been possible. Dr. Verma, as a co-director of the project has devoted her valuable time in this project, willingly. She has also prepared a Project Report on 'Leadership Style' which has already been published in book form. Presently, a number of Research Scholars are working under her supervision and besides her teaching, she is actively engaged in the different academic activities.

My thanks are also due to Dr. (Mrs) Geeta Gupta, Reader and Head, Department of English, who is also the Programme Officer of the Adult Education Programme of this college. In the capacity of an officer of the above programme she has inspired our students to collect data.

I thank my students particularly to those who have shown their enthusiasm in data collection. They have worked sincerely among the economically and socially backward women of Bhagalpur town. We are thankful to U.G.C. for financial assistance.

My thanks also go to Mr. Balkrishna Jha who has taken pain in typing the Project Report.

Principal   Anindita Mukherji
S.M. Mahavidyalaya
Bhagalpur

PREFACE

The problem of status of women has been studied widely and it has received wide attention from the different fields of researchers. One may find a vast literature on it as there has been considerable studies related to different aspects of women. However, there are limited publications concerning the women's education. Beginning the vedic ages to modern era, Education itself has been regarded as one of the most important contributors to emancipation of women. The importance of education can be pronounced by quoting the sayings of Mahatma Gandhi, 'You educate a man, you educate an individual, educate a woman, you educate a family.'

Therefore, it is assumed that with the spread of education among women, the women folk gradually become aware of the condition. Recently, governments (Central and State) is also making deliberate attempt to raise the status of women through its various developmental plans. Adult Education Programme is one of the major efforts in this direction.

Hence, this project was undertaken with a view to conduct a Survey on the women of Bhagalpur, particularly on those women who came under the adult education programme.

Besides this work on the above project our college also hold two National Seminars on women (a) 'LEGAL STATUS OF WOMEN IN INDIA' in August, 1984; (b) 'CONTRIBUTION OF WOMEN IN SCIENCE' in April 1986. Both Seminars were financed by the U.G.C. many eminent scholars participated in it and expressed their views regarding the different aspects of women. The major purpose of the first Seminar was to throw light on the women's condition because it was realised that still a systematic effort in this direction is needed.

The purpose of the Second Seminar was to highlight the work of women scientists in different fields.

The college has also undertaken a programme to bring out a bibliography of women scientists of India with their achievements.

Principal   Anindita Mukherji
S. Mahila Mahavidyalaya
Bhagalpur

CONTENTS

LIST OF TABLES AND FIGURES

CHAPTER I

INTRODUCTION

1. The Cultural Mileu

The role of women in the cultural development of society is underestimated and underscored in India. In Indian society, the concerted effort has been made to make the language, literature, art, science and technology all male oriented which indicate a negative attitude towards women. At the same time this attitude gives rise to the class structure in society. Besides, Indian society is primarily a fragmented society which never united its people on a Common Social cause, rather it differentiates people on their caste and class and even on the basis of their *gender i.e.*, male and female. In this context Wali (1984) has carefully remarked that in India, the cultural conditioning, and the socialization pattern, customs, rituals, traditions, value systems, religious ethos have been such and so different for male and female, that a female develops a voiceless minus personality (p. 179). Our culture also maintains that women should not be given power and their views should not be taken into account (Miller, 1981). However, this notion does not mar the traditional role of women where women have exerted enormous power through fostering the off-springs and have found this to be a valuable and gratifying activity. But only this gratification cannot provide them an equal status in the society.

2. Woman and Her Varied Status

The status of women can be discussed in the light of cultural set-up of India which provides a strong background.

In the beginning of the journey it would be wise to confess that since primitive stages to modern era, women have been looked upon as the second class citizens and they have always been treated as she

'cheap commodity' and not as the half part of the society (Women
Constitute nearly the 50% of the total population in India). So, the
overall status of women in India is low, even when the resources are
adequate.

In case of women the factors like, rural/urban background,
married/unmarried/widows, educated/uneducated, employed/unem-
ployed, etc. contribute least to their emancipation.

The general conclusions drawn on the basis of a number of
studies are :

> (a) The status of women in urban area is higher than the
> women of rural area.
> (b) The married women are ascribed greater status than the
> unmarried and widows.
> (c) The educated women enjoy better status than the uneducat-
> ed ones.
> (d) The working women are more privileged than the non-
> working.

In spite of a number of studies, the burning question of women's
emancipation still remains unanswered, because these findings are
not adequate. These studies do not throw light on the emancipation
of the whole mass, rather they have taken into account only one or
single aspect of women's area *i.e.* Social status, Economic status,
Legal status, Political status, etc., as if there are multiple statuses.
These statuses have emerged due to the sheer vastness contained
within the Indian society. It has also been reported that one cannot
speak of only one status for all women (Jones, 1980, p. 1) because
there are varieties of statuses which are dependent upon the caste,
class, religion, educational level, etc. Hence, in Indian society it is a
hard task to establish a national trait or national character of
women.

So the journey of confirmation of women's status is still incomplete and uncertain. One has to exert more and more if one aspires
to achieve the wishful thinking of equal status of women in all
respects. In this direction the studies related to the socio-economic
conditions of women will be more helpful in understanding the vital
issue of women status.

3. Status : As a Joint Function of Socio-economic Factors

The status of women in any society is determined by the interplay of various socio-economic factors. Some of these may be the 'objective' in nature, like education, employment, income, etc., or 'subjective' depending on the social values prevailing in the society. It is found that social status generally coincides with economic status. In other words, both are more or less overlapping. So, the sections which are economically very poor also occupy a low position in the social scale. So, it must be mentioned here that in the lower strata, the problems are more 'economic' than 'social'. Whereas in the 'middle' and 'upper' strata it is more 'social' than 'economic'.

In Indian society, the socio-economic status of women is usually determined by the position of her husband or family and her individual achievements were rarely considered. For example, a wife of a well placed man enjoyed higher status than a woman who was highly qualified and competent in her job. So, the 'ascribed status' dominated over 'achieved status' which was a part of the total social system. (Rao, 1983, p. 8)

4. Indices of Socio-economic Status

Since the overall status of a woman is a joint function of her socio-economic status, therefore, socio-economic status of women may be evaluated on the basis of a number of factors, such as caste and class, rural/urban background, family size, educational achievement and training received, the ratio of income/expenditure, freedom of choice in service and the occupational mobility.

To study the overall socio-economic condition of women four broad categories may be developed, *i.e.*,

    (*a*) Social Indicators
    (*b*) Educational Indicators
    (*c*) Economic Indicators
    (*d*) Other Indicators

Each category will include a number of relevant factors. However, there may be overlappings between the categories.

(*a*) *Social Indicators*

'There is a small section of brilliant women at the top of

politics, education, medicine, administration, public health, law, nursing, journalism, writing and advertising and the fine arts and just opposed with this bright picture is the great mass of Indian women who are illiterate and oppressed.' (Vedlankar, 1984, p. 17)

The above quotation explains that a few women have managed to acquire top positions in the different fields of specializations while the majority of women still lag behind due to their poor socio-economic condition. Some of the social indicators of their backwardness are as follows :

(i) Caste and Class

Low caste, low class dimension play important role in determining one's social condition in the society. In India, there are as many as 36 castes which have been divided into two broader categories i.e., forward and backward. These categories are further classified into Annexure I and Annexure II, which specify the different caste groups, like Schedule Caste, Schedule Tribes, etc. So far the caste is concerned it is presumed that women belonging to backward caste are socially more backward. So is the case with the class, because the problems of backwardness are more prominent in the lower class and to some extent in the middle class. The upper class ladies do not face such problems because their social positions in the society are well defined and well versed. The government programmes and scheme of Women Finance Corporation, Vocational Guidance Centres or Khadi Gramodyog Commission have done little to protect these women to stabilize their status.

(ii) Rural Urban Background

The most influential single determinant of the social status of any woman is her residence in an urban or rural setting. In rural setting the picture of woman is completely different because in rural areas, the ideal for women is set down by the ancient values and norms, like dutiful sacrificing unquestioning wife and a devoted mother. Family and regional practices further reinforce this role and therefore, there is little impetus for change of women's condition in rural areas. The changes are more perceptible in the urban regions and therefore, the relative condition of urban women is better than the rural.

(iii) Marital Status

In most cases the marital status and the social status are regarded as twins. Because it has been reported that in Indian society woman's status has generally been determined by the position of her husband and her individual achievements are rarely considered (text. p. 13). It is also pointed out that married women are accorded greater status than the unmarried and widowed. This phenomenon is more explicit in the social gatherings where even a best friend tries to avoid an unmarried female friend because he does not want to associate his name with her. This is just to save his public face. So in India, marriage is used as *protective shield* for both sexes, male as well as female.

While married women are regarded as auspicious persons, widowed women are inauspicious and are not welcome at religious rituals. Once a widow reaches very old age, she is accorded respect by virtue of her age regardless of her widowed status, but even then she does not present herself prominently at a wedding or another auspicious occasion (Manohar, 1980) widows of higher caste are required to observe mourning for a longer period with little or no hope of remarriage. Recently, this understanding is losing its weight and many remarriages are performed. But these are performed in joyless, simple function. On the other hand, the widower can celebrate his remarriage just after the thirteen days of mourning and with all preparations, as if the man was being married for the first time. This differential in ritual observances surrounding the widowhood of males and females is an eligent comment on the status of women *vis-a-vis* that of men.

(iv) Size of the Family

Number of family members or the size of the family also determines the social status. Here the running hypothesis is that the larger the family size the lower will be the status. Because most of the time the income of a family is relatively disproportionate to its expenditure and therefore, the status is placed at the lower end of the socio-economic scale. The bigger family size in the lower class people is due to their misconception that the greater number of siblings will add more money to the family and secondly, the people of lower socio-economic conditions are not aware of the various programmes of family planning. At the same time they do not want to spend money on the use of the contraceptives.

(v) Occupation

Occupation of women is a significant indicator. In India because the 70 per cent of the people live in rural areas, therefore, a large percentage of women are working as the agricultural sector. Majority of them are also engaged as coolie or labourer at the sites of building construction. While some of them earn their breads as maid servants. Tailoring, knitting, making papad, etc. are the major professions of urban class women because these women are mostly skilled labour, teaching in primary school and middle school is also common in the women of lower middle class. However, very few women are employed in private sector and public sector organization and if they are selected they are offered specific departments such as researh development and training. Because the jobs of personnel, administration, marketing are not allotted to them. Previously, working under a woman boss was taken as an havoc but now this phenomenon is gradually disappearing.

The purpose of the present study was to examine that to what extent the women of lower strata of Bhagalpur town are backward.

(b) Educational Indicators

'Education is the key that opens the door in life which is essentially social in character' (Hate, 1969). The level of education of women is an important indication for the understanding of the present and future status of women in a country. In spite of its unanimous role, it is being felt that education has not received its due attention, particularly in the case of women. Though Gandhijee has remarked long back that 'educating a man is educating an individual while educating a woman is educating a family', yet we find that in India, the literacy rate is very low.

Table 1 shows the literacy rates of males and females in India, both in rural and urban areas (Census of India, 1971). The index scores show the relative position of women as compared to men. The wide disparities between males and females are visible particularly in the rural areas. The Table also highlights the inter-State variations in the literacy rates.

Among the States and Union Territories the female literacy score is highest in Kerala and Chandigarh with 81 points followed by

TABLE 1

Literacy Rates* in India, by States and Union Territories, 1971

Sl. No.	States/Union Territories	TOTAL Index Score**			RURAL Index Score**				URBAN Index Score**		
		Female	Male	3 as % of 4	Female	Male	6 as % of 7		Female	Male	9 as % of 10
1	2	3	4	5	6	7	8		9	10	11
	India	18.70	39.45	47	18.17	33.76	54		42.14	61.28	69
1.	Andhra Pradesh	15.75	33.18	47	10.92	27.31	40		36.31	57.30	63
2.	Assam***	19.27	37.19	52	16.51	34.38	48		50.89	64.54	79
3.	Bihar	8.72	30.64	28	6.39	27.64	23		31.89	55.43	58
4.	Gujarat	24.75	46.11	54	17.19	38.92	44		44.77	63.96	70
5.	Haryana	14.89	37.29	40	9.24	32.57	28		41.48	59.12	70
6.	Himachal Pradesh	20.23	43.19	47	18.15	41.19	44		52.24	66.76	78
7.	Jammu and Kashmir	9.28	26.75	35	4.98	22.17	22		28.38	46.60	61
8.	Kerala	54.31	66.62	81	53.10	65.57	81		60.62	71.99	84
9.	Madhya Pradesh	10.92	32.70	33	6.10	27.05	23		36.98	66.46	56
10.	Maharashtra	26.43	51.04	52	17.84	43.22	41		47.33	66.88	71
11.	Manipur	19.53	46.04	42	16.35	43.04	38		40.43	65.80	61
12.	Meghalaya	24.56	34.12	72	18.94	27.68	68		59.69	69.93	85
13.	Mysore	20.97	41.62	50	14.54	35.40	41		41.61	60.40	69
14.	Nagaland	18.65	35.02	53	16.39	30.51	54		49.47	66.13	75
15.	Orissa	13.92	38.29	36	12.06	36.14	33		36.05	59.94	60

(Contd.)

TABLE 1 (Contd.)

1	2	3	4	5	6	7	8	9	10	11
16.	Punjab	25.90	40.38	64	19.88	34.69	57	45.41	58.55	78
17.	Rajasthan	8.46	28.74	29	4.03	22.87	18	29.69	55.53	53
18.	Tamil Nadu	26.64	51.78	52	18.98	45.14	42	45.42	66.76	68
19.	Tripura	21.19	40.20	53	17.27	36.43	47	55.03	72.42	76
20.	Uttar Pradesh	10.55	31.50	33	6.99	28.02	25	33.33	52.08	64
21.	West Bengal	22.42	42.81	52	15.02	35.80	42	47.84	62.01	77
	Union Territories									
1.	Andaman and Nicobar	31.11	51.64	60	25.66	46.80	55	51.85	66.93	77
2.	Arunachal Pradesh	3.71	17.82	21	3.00	15.77	19	31.18	59.28	53
3.	Chandigarh	54.35	66.97	81	18.34	38.84	47	57.89	70.03	84
4.	Dadar and Nagar Haveli	7.84	22.15	35	7.84	22.15	35	—	—	—
5.	Delhi	47.75	63.71	75	20.75	49.00	42	50.90	65.37	78
6.	Goa, Daman and Diu	35.09	54.31	65	31.06	50.40	62	47.21	64.39	73
7.	Laccadive, Minicoy and Amindivi Islands	30.56	56.38	54	30.56	56.48	54	—	—	—
8.	Pondicherry	34.62	57.29	60	25.87	51.14	51	46.60	65.83	71

* Literates/Population × 100

** Female Literacy as percentage of male literacy

*** Includes Union Territory of Mizoram

According to 1981 census the provisional literacy were as follows :

Persons	Male	Female
22,79,91,932	15,88,37,215	7,91,54,717.

Delhi. Bihar stands in the middle with 52 points. Literacy rates of females are much lower in the rural areas. Rural Bihar has got only 48 points while this point is 79 for urban areas.

It seems that the education has received wide attention in urban areas. Yet from a comparative stand point that educational indices of Indian women are far behind, because the 'Social attitudes to girl's education vary from acceptance to absolute indifference'. (Vedalankar, 1984)

For the present purpose, the educational indicators will include the following aspects of education :

     (*i*) Respondent's own educational level
    (*ii*) Her father's education
   (*iii*) Training received (if any)
   (*iv*) The adult education programme for women

(*i*) *Respondent's Own Educational Level*

Since the respondents of the present study are women of lower class, therefore, it is assumed that there will be very little or no education among them. The hypothesis will be further substantiated by the obtained data which are presented in Chapter III.

(*ii*) *Father's Education*

Here, it is expected that even in the people of lower class there will be some basic education. The father being a male sex is thought to have received at least primary education *i.e.*, below matric. On the contrary, the female sex (the daughter) of the same family is not privileged with this opportunity.

(*iii*) *Training Received*

The area of the present survey is proper Bhagalpur town where generally the women of urban population reside. As mentioned earlier, urban women enjoy more facilities and in urban localities there are greater scope for their training.

In each town of Bihar including Bhagalpur a number of training centres are operating at the cost of the government, like doll-making centre, tailoring and sewing centre, wool weaving and knitting centre, weaving of raw silk, weaving of bed covers and carpets and household training centres. In most of the training programmes, the trainees also receive a stipend for a particular period. Later on, they may be appointed for a low paid part-time or full-time job.

Apart from these training centres, there are other business too, for example, papad and potato chips making, community kitchen, poultry farm, growing vegetables, making paper covers, etc.

Here, our task is to locate the number and percentage of those women who have received training under these governmental schemes.

(iv) Adult Education Programme for Women

The present age is an advanced age of technological development which demands change in every direction. To keep in step with this changing society, education is the only answer. The acute necessity for adult education has been widely recognized by the world today for all round socio-economic development. All development schemes are incomplete if they have no reference to the female population of the area. Hence it was accepted that a certain level of literacy was to be achieved by every women irrespective of their background whether rural or urban. In this direction the government policy of widespread informal education is the most gallantry effort.

By its definition and purpose, adult education is the acquisition of new ideas, skills, attitudes and understanding by people whose primary occupation in life is other than learning or studentship. In content therefore, it deals with all problems of man and society, in scope it covers all population, except that part of it which belongs to school, colleges and vocational institutions, and in form, it is an variegated as life itself. (Singh, 1957, p. 1)

The above statement gives wider picture of adult education programme initiated by the government. One of the major objectives of this programme is the development of urban women, because there is a growing realization that culture and civilization of a country largely depends upon the urban people since urban people influence the day-to-day administration and in tune are influenced by the factors of urbanization, therefore, it is essential to keep their minds sound. Hence, it is asserted that the urban people need Adult Education most and their motivation of it is the greatest.

For women in urban areas a higher level of education would be necessary. The needs and opportunities for reading are greater in the urban areas and consequently the urban women would need a greater fluency in reading. Therefore, a different (of high standard) syllabi should be prepared for the urban women.

In adult education programme for women there is provision for condensed courses. The scheme consists of providing two years training of mature women between the ages 20 and 35. These courses are run by the voluntary agencies having adequate experience and background of educational work. They are financed by the Central Social Welfare Board.

Now a days, Universities are also taking active participation in organising programmes for informal education, such as, expansion lectures, forums, discussion groups, seminars, conferences, etc. Besides, in most of the colleges a programme officer of Adult Education has been appointed by the University who is supposed to look after ten (10) centres. One such University is the Jamia Millia where the Institute of Adult Education known as Idara Talim-O-Taraqqi was established in 1938. 'The objective of the institute was to discover ways and means of making adult education an integral part of community life, to prepare literature and teaching aids and draw up a syllabus for the training of workers' (Mohsini, 1973, p. 26). A part of Karol Bagh, Delhi was selected for the field work and a centre was opened there. On the basis of the experience drawn from the centre, the Idara drew up a scheme of education centre with projects and various programmes. It also prepared a number or booklets in various objects and some other literature and teaching aids for adult and mass education. In this way, the Jamia Millia was the first and foremost University which took the trouble of spreading mass education among the illiterate. In Bhagalpur, our college is no exception. In our college too, we have adult education programme officer and a number of students are working under her leadership. She is the incharge of 10 centres which are located in the proper town. In each centre, thirty to forty females are enrolled.

The adult education programme is beneficial in the sense that it provides employment to a large number of females either at supervisory level, or as Project Officer. Secondly women are given opportunity to utilize their time and energy. Apart from this the feeling of a meaningful life gives them self-confidence and psychological satisfaction.

In summing up, the education of women is fundamental for the achievement and for their legal and social independence. Although the educated women are not clear about their role expectations. Yet let us hope that their educational level and training will bring new awareness in them which in turn will help the nation in building a strong national character.

Our major concern is to see whether the adult education centres of Bhagalpur town are meeting its targets or not.

(c) Economic Indicators

The role of women in the economic development of a nation has always been underestimated. The economic problems of Indian women are more severe than their female counterparts all over the world. It is chiefly because women are not treated at par with men. 'The economic disparity and economic inequality between men and women are inherent in the relations among people such as super ordination and subordination.' (Nandi, 1984).

The basic question is that to what extent the women accept their impoverished economical condition.

The economic condition of women may constitute a host of factors. These indicators specify the area in which the women are financially backward. Some such indicators of economic backwardness in women are :

   (i) Income
   (ii) Nature and type of expenditure

(*iii*) Service orientation

(*iv*) Government aid

By Constitution, the economic position of Indian women is not sound. In India, the property rights are not conducive to women's condition because they have not given any economic independence. Even if it is legally accepted, it is only in theory and not in practice. So, women do not inherit even her husband's property as they have hardly any right on property. It is primarily due to the notion that women do not possess a separate identity, therefore, she would not require separate property (Gulati, 1985, p. 256). After the death of the husband, property ultimately goes to the son and even the properties are under her name, properties are managed by the male members of the family. In some cases the ornaments which are considered as the 'personal property' of the wife are captured by her son and daughter-in-law because she is economically dependent upon them.

(*i*) *Income*

The first and foremost indicator of a woman's economic condition is her income. The problem of per capita income is more acute in the women of lower strata where women earn their income out of the economic necessity. Therefore, they opt for a job where there is no social security, no pension and no long term financial benefits. They are mostly engaged in as unskilled labour coolies or in self-employment. These women are compelled to take up such jobs in order to meet her ends. They just cannot afford the luxury of staying at home. Due to the economical compulsion they cannot adhere to the rigid social values. The man and woman work together and they lead a community life.

It has been reported that 58.5% women opted for a job out of economic pressure (Talwar, 1984, p. 40). Rao has also observed that the higher work participation rate does not go with the high literacy rate, which indicates the economic backwardness of lower class women. Findings also indicate that the total income of this group, in any case, does not exceed Rs. 500/- per month.

(*ii*) *Nature and Type of Expenditure*

The economic condition of a woman also depends on the nature and type of expenditure which will include.

(1) Joint expenditure
(2) Self-dependent, and
(3) Hardship

(*1*) *Joint Expenditure* : Joint expenditure refers to those families where the number of earners are more than one and the earners spend their income jointly. It has been assumed that due to the large family size the number of earners in one family may vary from 1 to 7 or more. A majority of working women (71.3%) belonged to such families as had 2-3 earning members while there was only 16.7% family who have only one earning member (Talwar. 1984, p. 18) *i.e.* the respondent herself. Here it is presumed that if a family adopts the joint expenditure system then there will be greater scope for meeting the demands of the family because irrespective of their equal contribution their demands remain uneffected.

(*2*) *Self-dependent* : But due to urbanization most of the joint families are broken down into nuclear families and therefore, people in general and women in particular have become self-dependent. Most of the single woman earns for her livings. This indicates that these women are dependent on their own earnings only. But in the women of lower strata the percentage of this sort of expenditure is very rare, because women of this class generally lead a community life.

(*3*) *Hardship* : If a woman reports that she has difficulties in running the household or she has to take loan from others, or she cooks only one time a day, then this will indicate her economic backwardness.

(*iii*) *Service Orientation*

It has been widely accepted that the low class women opt for a job out of their bare necessities. So, the degree of service orientation would be greater in these women. The two major dimensions of service orientation may be the (*A*) Desire for service (*B*) Choice of service. The former is simple and easy because one has only to gather information regarding her desires *i.e.*, whether a woman aspires for a job or not? While the later one, the choice of service is more complicated because in our situation, the choice of service is very limited. In fact, there is no choice. There are a host of factors which limit the choice, such as limitations of the family, norms, place of work, distance in kilometre, nature of work, service condition, and payment etc. act as detrimental to women's taking up a job. Above all, if a woman gets a job then she is paid low wages even if she is working for equal number of hours. So the wage discrimination is also one of the major obstacles in the choice of service.

In spite of the strong desire for service one cannot find a suitable job because women of low class have to face multiple problems, like ignorance, illiteracy, lack of skills, seasonal nature of employment, heavy physical work, long hours of work with limited payment, lack of wage guarantee, job security and lack of minimum facilities at the work place, ill treatment migration, alienation, etc. Although the working condition or general work climate is very impoverished yet a number of women continue to search and finally take-up their jobs for their livelihood (Manohar, 1980). So the problem of choice of service is more intense at the lower strata of women because they have to take-up a job, out of the economic compulsions.

(iv) Government Aid

The need of the hour is a 'positive desire' to help the less fortunate women. Though it is a tremendous task yet government is trying its best to provide some financial support (in cash or in kinds) especially to women of lower strata. A number of loan schemes have been proposed by the government to diminish the imbalances. Here, our task is to see that what percentage of women receive this loan and how far these schemes are successful in granting loan to the women ?

(d) Other Indicators

One of the important indicators of socio-economic backwardness may be the nature and type of activities in which the women pass their time. If the daily activities are productive and constructive then this will bring efficiency to them and in turn it may add to their family income. So, my humble submission would be that one should learn the techniques of time saving and time management and then only one can utilize her time for extra work, like tailoring, sewing, community kitchen, part-time job of nursing, etc., for which a little training is required. Therefore, apart from their household work, women can engage themselves in more productive activities which may ultimately solve their economic backwardness.

Because there are overlappings between social and economic indicators, therefore, it is very difficult to segregate the socio-economic problems of women as social and economic. Hence an attempt has been made to study this consolidated problem with the help of a number of relevant indicators which have been classified under different categories such as, social educational and economic indicators.

CHAPTER II

PURPOSE AND METHODOLOGY

SECTION I

Purpose

Since past few years, our college has been making constant effort to throw light on the status of women. To bring the women's condition in lime light it held two National Seminars on Women. Both the seminars—(a) Legal Status of women in India (August, 1984) and (b) Contribution of women in Science (April, 1986) were sponsored by U.G.C. Many Scholars participated in the Seminar and discussed women's contribution in the various field of science including Psychology and Home Science. A volume on 'Legal Status of Women' has already been edited by the college and the volume on 'Contribution of Women to Science' is waiting for publication. Both the volumes on women's status and their contribution included a large number of relevant papers which were presented in the different sessions of Seminars. Recently, we are looking forward for the establishment of a *Centre for Advance Study for Women* here, in our college.

So far the present research work is concerned this study may be taken as a joint venture of the college. This small piece of research was started with a view to conduct a survey on the women of Bhagalpur town, particularly of those women who came under the Adult Education Programme.

The major purpose of the present study was to gather relevant data regarding the socio-economic condition of the women who are below poverty tune.

The variables under study were categorized into four broad categories :

1. Social Indicators
    (*a*) Caste and class
    (*b*) Rural/Urban background
    (*c*) Marital status
    (*d*) Size of the family
    (*e*) Occupation

2. Educational Indicators
    (*a*) Respondent's own education
    (*b*) Respondent's father's education
    (*c*) Training received
    (*d*) The Adult Education Programme for women

3. Economic Indicators
    (*a*) Income
    (*b*) Nature and type of Expenditure
    (*c*) Service orientation
    (*d*) Government Aid.

4. Other Indicators
Nature and type of daily activities.

Excepting a few, most of variables had sub-categories which will be discussed later in this chapter (Section-II, 'Measures', p. 21).

SECTION II

Methodology

(*a*) Sample

The sample of the present study included 240 women of Bhagalpur town. These women belong to the financially backward section of the society, who came under the Adult Education Scheme.

The age range of the women sample was between 15 to 34 and above. But out of 240 only 3 (three) women were in the age range of 34 and above which is only the marginal part (1.25%) of the total population. While there were 130 women between the age range of 15-24 (54.17%) and 107 women (44.58%) were in the age group of 25-34 (see Table 2),

TABLE 2
Sample : Frequency and Percentage of Age

Age Range	Frequency	Percentage
15-24	130	54.17
24-34	107	44.58
34 and above	3	1.25
Total	240	100.00

(b) *Research Setting*

The setting for the present research work was the proper town of Bhagalpur. The major pre-condition of the setting selection was to cover only those localities which come under the Adult Education Programme of this college. It is relevant to note that there are ten centres of Adult Education for which one programme officer has been appointed by the Bhagalpur University. In our college Dr. (Mrs.) Geeta Gupta (Head, English Department) is the Programme Officer of the Adult Education Programme who is supposed to look after the centres. These centres are located in different parts of Bhagalpur town. Such as, Bhikhanpur, Chhoti Khanjarpur, Badi Khanjarpur, Parwatti, etc. For the present purpose all the centres were selected, but out of the ten only eight centres returned the filled questionnaire. So, two centres of this programme are automatically excluded from the study.

(c) *General Description of Bhagalpur Town*

Bhagalpur, one of the B-grade cities of Bihar is located at the eastern part of its capital town. Just like its capital, it is also located at the bank of Ganges. The total population of Bhagalpur town is 2 lakhs and 21 thousand with an area of 5,589 square kilometre. This town has its old Jain culture where most of the residents are business class people. Marwari, Bengali and Muslims communities constitute majority of the population.

Bhagalpur is famous for semi-culture institutes which are located at Nathnagar and Champanagar. Nearly 5,000 to 10,000 weavers earn their livings by weaving of raw silk, pure silk by weaving carpets, etc. Bed covers, shirt piece, suits, lungis are the main products of weaving centres.

Like other leading town, Bhagalpur has its own recognized

University which was established in the year 1960. In this town we have medical college known as Bhagalpur Medical College and Hospital (B.M.C.H.), Engineering College and Sabour Agriculture College. The well known Vikramshila University is also nearer to this town.

The serene water of Gange of Sultanganj another subdivision within Bhagalpur is used for worshipping Lord Shiva of Deoghar during the month of August *i.e., Shravan.* In this sense it is considered as a religious place. Tourists from different parts of India drop in here to worship Lord Shiva of Deoghar.

The newly commissioned National Thermal Power Corporation (N.T.P.C.) in Kahalgaon is one of the greatest achievements of Bhagalpur town. The N.T.P.C. is supposed to generate power in the year 1987-88.

Various developmental programmes have been started here. Adult Education Programme and Angan Badi Centres are prominent among them. These centres provide extensive employment to as many as 2,000 women.

Though the civic condition of Bhagalpur is not very good and the rate of crime is still very high, yet Bhagalpur is known for its own culture with its specific historical importance (see Figure I and Figure II).

TABLE 3
Rural-Urban Composition of Bhagalpur Population
[Population 1981 census]

Total	Rural	Urban
2,610,719	2,307,330	303,389

The Table indicates that according to 1981 census the total population of Bhagalpur is 26,10,719. Out of which 23,07,330 persons reside in rural areas while only 3,03,389 people live in urban areas.

The census reports also reveal that the percentage of urban

population to total population was 10.61 in 1971 and 11.62 in 1981.

TABLE 4

Description of Literate Population in Rural-Urban Areas of Bhagalpur

[Literate population 1981 census]

	Persons	*Males*	*Females*
Total	7,16,635	5,19,941	1,96,694
Rural	5,61,515	4,19,668	1,41,847
Urban	1,55,120	1,00,273	54,847

The Table reveals that the total literates population of Bhagalpur district is 7,16,635. The literacy rate in male population is 5,19,941 and in female population it is 1,96,694.

Similarly, in rural areas the literacy among male is 4,19,668 and the literacy among rural females is only 1,41,847. However, the situation is little better in urban areas where out of 1,55,120 persons, 1,00,273 males are literate while only 54,847 urban women have been found to be literate.

In 1981 census, it has also been reported that the percentage of male and female workers in Bhagalpur are 85 per cent and 15 per cent respectively. Out of which the figure for agricultural sector is quite impressive as 80.02 per cent population are engaged in agricultural sector while only 19.98 per cent population are engaged in non-agricultural sector.

(d) Measures

A structured interview schedule was prepared by the Co-Director of the project. The items of the schedule measure the socio-economic condition of women. Most of the items were in Yes/No format while there were descriptive items too. The items measure the fundamental indicators of Socio-Economic condition. Such as caste, education, occupation, social status, income, expenditure, rural/urban background, number of family members etc. Except a few most of the variables had their sub-categories *e.g.* there were four items in service orientation,

Service Orientation

Similarly there were three items for the variable Nature and Type of expenditure for example :

Nature and Type of Expenditure

There were altogether 35 items in the schedule.

(e) Procedure

The data were collected in the class room situation in Adult Education centres. The schedules were distributed among and respondents of each centre and the respondents were asked to fill up the schedule in the presence of the Supervisor and the Instructor of their units. As mentioned earlier there were ten centres, out of which only eight centres participated in the study. Each centre completed the 30 schedules while two centres did not respond to it. In this way altogether 240 schedules were retained for the data analysis.

CHAPTER III

RESULT AND DISCUSSION

An Overview

The purpose of the present study was to examine the degree of socio-economic backwardness among the lower class women of Bhagalpur town. Data were gathered regarding the different indicators of socio-economic backwardness which were classified into four broad categories *i.e.*, social, educational, economic and others. Each category also included a number of sub-categories.

In the present research only frequency and percentage could be obtained hence The tables are being prepared accordingly. However, the data were entered into a second phase analysis which produced specific results. (Section II)

Section I of this chapter throws light on the frequency and percentage of each variable while *Section II* is about the relative percentage of each variable with other relevant variables.

SECTION I

As many as ten to twelve Tables have been presented in this section which are placed according to the serial order of the variables.

1. Social Indicators

There were only five indicators of social status of women *i.e.*, (*a*) Caste and class (*b*) Rural-urban background (*c*) Marital status (*d*) Family size and (*e*) Occupation.

TABLE 5
Caste : Frequency and Percentage

Caste	Frequency	Percentage
Forward	22	90.79
Backward	217	9.21
Total	239	100.00

The Table suggested that out of 239 women only 22 women (9.21) belonged to forward caste while the majority of them belonged to the backward caste group. The percentage of backward women was 90.97%. Since the low caste, low class dimension is itself an indicator of the low social status, therefore, our assumption regarding the low social status of lower class women is confirmed by the obtained data.

No separate Table was prepared for the rural-urban back-ground of women because this survey was conducted on the women of Bhagalpur town. Hence the total number constituted the urban population.

TABLE 6
Marital Status : Frequency and Percentage

Marital Status	Frequency	Percentage
Unmarried	73	30.42
Married	160	66.66
Widow	7	2.92
Total	240	100.00

In any class, the most important phenomenon of one's status is her marital condition, *i.e.*, whether a woman is married, unmarried or widow. The results revealed that more than 50% women were married (66.66%) while 30.42% women were unmarried and a very low percentage of women constitutes the third category *i.e.* widow, the percentage of widow women even in lower class is only 2.92%.

This suggests that the social status of these women are not affected by their marital status rather it indicates an improved social status because in Indian society, the married women are ascribed higher status than others.

Marital status also included items regarding the respondent's stay either with her own parents with her husband or with her in-laws family. A separate Table has been provided for their pattern of living.

TABLE 7

Marital Status : Collectivism *vs.* Individualism : Frequency and Percentage

Marital Status	Staying with her own parents	Staying with husband	Staying with in-laws family
Yes			
Frequency	49	149	108
Percentage	25.39	77.20	56.84
No			
Frequency	144	44	82
Percentage	74.61	22.80	43.16

The Table showed that the larger percentage of women live with her husband, *i.e.* 77.20 per cent while only 25.39 per cent women live with her own parents and more than half population 56.84 per cent live with their husband along with the family of their in-laws.

In general results indicated that in India the collectivist orientation is gradually losing its charm as people are moving towards individualism, *i.e.*, living with her husband only. However, this is not true to the whole population because the half of the population still lives with the members of their in-laws family.

TABLE 8

Family Members : Frequency and Percentage

Family members	Frequency	Percentage
1 to 9	202	91.82
10 or Above	18	8.82
Total	220	100.00

The majority of the women have a range of 1 to 9 members in a family. The percentage of this family size was very high *i.e.*, 91.82 while a very low percentage reported a family size of ten or more than 10 members.

The results suggested that even in lower class women, the large family size is not encouraged.

TABLE 9

Occupation : Frequency and Percentage

Occupation	Frequency	Percentage
Service	28	11.67
Business	212	88.33
Total	240	100.00

On the basis of the above data two sub-categories were developed *i.e.*, Service and Business. Here it was found that a large percentage of lower class women (88.33 per cent) were engaged in *business* while only 11.67 per cent were the *service class women.*

The high rate of business suggests that in the lower class women there is less scope of employment. Therefore, they engage themselves in some sort of business just to add income to her family.

2. Educational Indicators

There were only four indicators in this category *i.e.*, (a) Respondent's own education (b) Respondent's father's education (c) Training received and (d) Adult education.

TABLE 10

Level of Education : Frequency and Percentage

Level of Education	Respondents own education	Respondent's father's education
Below matric (Illiterate)		
Frequency	240	215
Percentage	100	89.58%
Above Matric		
Frequency	00	24
Percentage	00%	10%
Above graduation		
Frequency	00	1
Percentage	00%	0.42%

The figure of level of education is very depressive because all the women (N=240) were illiterate. So the illiteracy rate was hundred per cent in respondent's own education.

The case was somewhat different in father's education where 10 per cent fathers were above matric and only one father was graduate. But majority of them (89.58 per cent) were below matric like their daughters.

The results suggested that in lower class not only the women were illiterate but the majority of them were also illiterate. Therefore, the low level of education supports our standing assumption of educational backwardness in lower class people. No Table has been prepared for the indicator training because women have not reported about their training courses.

TABLE 11
Adult Education : Frequency and Percentage

Adult Education	Frequency	Percentage
Yes	222	99.17
No	2	83
Total	224	100.00

The adult education programme has yielded a very impressive figure as 99.17 per cent women have reported that they are receiving adult education while only a negligible percentage. 83 per cent reported that they are not receiving any educational facilities.

The result highlights the positive side of the coin *i.e.*, the facilities of adult education is available to each and every woman of lower class hence they are raising their educational standard through it.

So, the government policy of development of women in rural as well as in urban areas is most successful and its implementation is also satisfactory. Hence one cannot deny the fact that most of the centres of this programme have achieved its targets. On the whole adult education programme is the most successful programmes which helps the illiterate to become aware of their surroundings.

3. Economic Indicators

The major indicators of economic status were (a) Income (b) Nature and type of expenditure (c) Service orientation and (d) Government Aid.

TABLE 12
Income : Frequency and Percentage

Income	Frequency	Percentage
Below 500	175	72.92
Above 500	65	27.08
Total	240	100.00

The above Table showed that out of 240 women 175 were earning an income which is below 500; this group is the larger group which constitutes the 72.92 per cent of the total population while only 27.08 per cent women were in the 500 or above 500.

The result straightaway indicates the financial back-wardness among the women of lower class because majority of them are below poverty line.

TABLE 13
Nature and Type of the Expenditure : Percentage Only

Nature and type of Expenditure	Joint expenditure	Self-dependent	Hardship
Yes Percentage	81%	24.78%	44.14%
No Percentage	19%	75.22%	55.86%
Total	100%	100%	100%

As we know the nature and type of expenditure is one of the major indicators of economic backwardness. This indicator was measured through three items *i.e.*, (a) joint expenditure (b) Self-dependent and (c) hardship. The Table suggested that 81 women were spending their income jointly while 24.78% were self-dependent on their income. The Table also revealed that 44.14% women reported that they are not facing any financial difficulties. Table also explains that the 55.86% women had to face financial difficulties so their financial position was not comfortable.

The results highlight the following conclusions : (a) Majority of lower class women earn jointly and spend jointly which help the women in meeting their basic needs. (b) Only a small percentage of women are self-dependent. (c) More than 50% women reported that they face hardship.

TABLE 14

Service Orientation : Percentage Only

Service Orientation	Desire for service	Choice of service in urban area
Yes Percentage	50%	51.60%
No Percentage	50%	48.40%
Total	100	100

This Table was about the service orientation among the women of lower class. The Table suggested that in each category there were 50% women. This meant that 50% women expressed the desire for service and other 50% did not. Similarly there is no remarkable difference in their choice of service. That is only 51.60% women reported that they can go to either urban or rural area for job. While near about 50% i.e. 48.40% women reported that they do not want to move for their job.

So, there is only 50% population who opted for either service or for occupational mobility.

4. Other Indicators

Some indicators which do not come under any other specific headings have been grouped under the heading of 'other indicators'.

One of them is the *Nature and type of activities* in which the women are engaged in. The major occupation or activities among the women of lower class is their *Home work i.e.*, the 58.82 per cent. The next larger group constitutes the women who are engaged in *other work* while only 11.76 per cent women reported that they are doing knitting and sewing.

TABLE 15

Nature and Type of Activities : Frequency and Percentage

Daily work	Frequency	Percentage
Home work	50	58.82
Knitting and sewing	10	11.76
Other work	25	29.42
Total	85	100.00

Therefore, the results suggested that the major activities in which the majority of women are engaged is their *Home work*.

It is due to the fact that most of the women do not get time for other work, therefore, they are fully engaged in domestic work so these women should learn the technique of time savings.

TABLE 16

Government Aid : Frequency and Percentage

Government Aid	Frequency	Percentage
Yes	12	5%
No	228	95%
Total	240	100%

A very marginal percentage reported that they have received any government aid. Because the 95 per cent women reported that they have not received any financial assistance from the government.

This indicates the failure of the government in providing financial aid to the poor women. It also explains that the different schemes of government aid are only on paper and not in practice. It means that the government agencies are not working properly.

So there is an urgent need of mobilising the government resources in right direction.

SECTION II

The second phase analysis of the data produced in the following Tables 17 to 22. In each Table one single variable was compared with its other relevant variables. The overall percentage of each variable have been reported in each Table. So in second phase analysis an attempt was made to predict one single variable. For example caste, occupation, education, etc., separate Table has been provided for each variable.

Table 17 reveals that there were only 22 women in forward caste while as many as 217 women were in backward caste group. The relative percentage of different variables yielded the following results :

(a) In both castes forward and backward the 82.0 per cent and 72.72 per cent women reported a family size of 0 to 9 members. While only 5.99 and 4.55 women had a family size of ten or more than ten members.

The result indicates that the family size is independent of the caste group whether it is forward or backward.

(b) So far the *occupation* is concerned the trend was not similar. In forward caste as there was a high percentage of service class *i.e.*, 27.27 per cent while it was only 9.38 in backward caste. However, the percentage of business was much higher in backward caste *i.e.*, 99.55 but it was only 9.68 in forward caste group.

The higher percentage of business in backward caste suggests that the women of backward group are not fit for any job, therefore, they are engaged in several business. It also indicates their greater backwardness.

(c) The percentage of income is almost similar as 27.27 per cent and 22.73 per cent forward women have reported a monthly income of below Rs. 500 and above Rs. 500. However, a sharp difference in percentage was observed in the monthly income of backward women where 42.50 women belonged to the low income group *i.e.*, below 500 while only 17.98 per cent women backward caste earn in income of above Rs. 500.

The higher percentage of women in low income group indicate the greater financial backwardness caste.

TABLE 17

Caste and Other Relevant Variables : Percentage Only

Caste	Family members		Occupation		Income		Nature and type of expenditure		Service Orientation			Govt. Aid	Level of Edn.	
	0-0	10 or above	Ser-vice	Busi-ness	Below 500	Above 500	Joint	Self dependent	Hard-ship for service	Desire for service	Choice for service		Own Father's Edn.	Adult Edn.
FORWARD 122	88.01	5.99	27.27	7.38	27.27	22.73	90.90	18.18	36.36	59.10	50	4.54 00%	1. 72 2. 22.73 3. 4.55	72 86 4.55
BACKWARD 217	72.72	4.55	9.68	99.55	42.80	17.98	78.80	17.52	39.63	49.31	43.32	5.52 00%	1. 93.53 2. 6.45	77 6.45

Education : 1. Stand for Illiterate
2. For above matric
3. For above graduate

(d) The percentage of *Joint expenditure* was almost similar in both caste groups *i.c.*, 90.90 and 78.80. In both castes only 17 to 18 per cent women were *self-dependent* while 36.86 and 39.63 women reported that they are facing economical problems in their households. So, in both groups, the trend of *nature* and *type* of *expenditure* was almost similar. The findings indicate that even today, the Indians are more collectivists as they cling to their ingroups and spend their income jointly.

(e) The variable *desire for service* and choice of service did not yield any marked difference. The percentage for desire for service in forward caste was 59.10 and it was 49.31 in backward caste. Similarly, the percentage of choice of service in rural/urban places in both caste groups were 50 per cent and 43.32 per cent respectively.

The data did not provide any logical base for two variable *caste* and *service orientation*.

(f) So far the government aid is concerned the percentage was almost equal in both caste groups *i.e.*, 4.54 and 5.32.

So neither caste received more financial aid from the government. It indicates to an impartial attitude on the part of the government in providing financial aid.

(g) The level of education was measured through three items—

    (i) respondent's own educational level
    (ii) father's education and
    (iii) adult education.

In both castes, the level of *own education* was very poor as the respondents (N=22, N=217) were all illiterate. In case of *fathers education* the figures were not very bright as in forward caste 72.72 per cent and in backward caste 93.53 per cent fathers were illiterate. The level of father's education was slightly better in forward caste where 22.73 per cent fathers were *matriculate* and 4.55 were *graduates*. The percentage of adult education programme was almost equal in both caste groups. The relative percentage were 86.36 and 77.42.

Though the findings of educational level reveal a slightly better condition of education in forward caste yet it is not up to the mark,

Table of occupation (Table 18) shows that occupation-wise only 27 women were in service while a large number of women (N = 217) were engaged in several business.

The following results were obtained :

(a) In service as well as in business class the 70.37 and 70.15 women had a family size of 0 to 9 members while rest 29.63 and 29.25 had a family size of ten or more than ten members.

(b) In both groups service and business, the illiteracy rate among the respondents was hundred per cent. However, the percentage of illiteracy of *father's education* was high in business class women i.e., 93.36 while it was 55.55 in service class women. In business class only 6.13 per cent fathers were matriculate while the percentage of fathers education was relatively high in service class women i.e., 44.74. The percentage of graduate father was nil in business class but it was 3.70 in service class women. In both groups equal percentage was obtained in the case of adult education.

The results indicate that the service class women had a better educational background where some matriculate and graduate fathers were located.

(c) The two classes also differ in their monthly income as the 44.44 women of service class reported a monthly income of 500 or above while only 12.32 per cent women of business class had a income of Rs. 500 or above. The percentage of monthly income was relatively low in business class.

(d) The business class women also showed a high percentage of joint *expenditure* i.e., 80.10% while the percentage of joint expenditure was relatively low in service class i.e., 59.25%. The percentage of *self-dependent* was also higher in business class (25.11) while it was just half in service class women (11.11). The most interesting result was obtained in the case of *Hardship* when 48.15 per cent women of service class reported about their financial crisis, while the problem of financial crisis was less severe in business class women. The result indicated that the service class

TABLE 18

Occupation and Other Relevant Variables : Percentage Only

Name of the variables occupation	Family members		Education		Income		Nature and type of expenditure			Service orientation		Government Aid
	0-9	10 or above	Own Father's Edn.	Adult Edn.	Below 500	500 or above	Joint	Self dependent	Hardship for service	Desire for service	Choice for service	
Service N=27	70.37	29.63	100% 1. 55.55 2. 40.74 3. 3.70	92.59	33.70	44.44	59.25	11.11	48.15	55.55	48.15	3.70
Business N=211	70.15	29.85	100% 1.93.36 2. 6.13	93.36	38.38	12.32	80.10	25.11	39.81	49.70	43.60	5.69

. women have reported the low percentage of joint expenditure and high percentage of *Hardship*. On contrary, the business women have reported high percentage of hardship joint expenditure and lower percentage of hardship.

The above findings support the investigators assumption that the problem of hardship will be more severe in those families where there is low percentage of joint expenditure. It is chiefly due to the fact that in joint expenditute, the household is managed jointly which is mostly irrespective of the equal contribution of each member, therefore, in joint expenditure even if an individual earns less it does not matter much as the basic needs of each member of the family are fulfilled.

(*e*) In case of service orientation the two classes did not show sharp differences. Both the classes. (service and business) were almost equal on the dimensions *i.e.*, (*a*) desire for service and (*q*) choice of service.

(*f*) However, a high percentage of business class women received the government aid *i.e.*, 5.69. It is a fine attempt on the part of the government which is extending loans particularly to the poor women for their small scale business.

Table 19 shows that there were as many as 202 women with a family size of 0 to 9 members while only 18 women had a family size of ten of more than ten members.

Table 19 reveals the following specific results :

(*a*) The higher percentage of women had an income of less than Rs. 500. However, 24.25 members of small family and 5.55 per cent women of large family size had an earning of Rs. 500 or above that.

(*b*) The phenomenon of *joint expenditure* was prominent in both groups as the relative percentages were 82.17 and 100 per cent. Further the percentage of hardship was lower in the larger family size *i.e.*, 22.22 while it was almost double in small family, *i.e.*, 41.58. The percentage of *self-dependent* was low in large family while it was 22.77 in the family size of zero to nine members.

(a) It was interesting to note that the women of larger family size were very anxious for service (22.22) and choice of service (11.11). The percentage is relatively small in small family service (5.44) and (48.51).

This indicates that the women of small family sizes are more pessimistic in the sense that in the small family mostly they look for jobs and service even if they have to change of place.

(b) It is also interesting to note that the small family size have received service and choice in lower percentage of government aid and choice (5.44).

Therefore, in general, the findings suggest that the women of small family size are more pessimistic and that is why they serve to help, they prefer hardship and they prefer service orientation.

The family expenditure (82.17) of ... the dependent on family members is ... small family. The choice of self depended rate of the better-less education was less percentage of nuclear families was ... family. Thus on the average, the ... dismissed that there were less expenditure as the dependent on ... spreading with children.

Following observations were made in the level of education.

(a) The respondent's own educational standard as influences the percentage of small family size was less... variable and is (82.17). The results of such education are clear on the mean literacy and the percentage of joint family expenditure is (82.17) and (24.25). However they could come to conclude ... in case of nuclear families. Thus the percentage of small family was (38.11) while the above percentage of joint family are economic Delhi.

The findings suggest that the women who had no education have develop more pessimistic family planning and therefore joint family ... have a small family size in the joint family will help the women to overcome their socio-economic backwardness.

TABLE 19
Family members and other Relevant Variables : Percentage Only

Name of the variables	Income		Nature and type of expenditure		Service orientation			
	Below 500	Above 500	Joint expenditure	Self dependent	Hardship	Desire for service	Choice of service	Government Aid
Size 0-9 N=202	38.11	24.25	82.17	22.77	41.58	55.95	48.51	5.44
10 and Above N=18	5.55	5.55	100%	00%	22.22	22.22	11.11	Nil

(c) It was surprising to note that the women of larger family size were low on desire for service (22.22) and choice of service (11.11). The percentage was relatively high in small family size (55.95 and 48.51).

This indicates that the women of small family size are more pragmative in the sense that despite their small family they look for job and even they are ready for change of place.

(d) It is also interesting to note that the 5.44 women of small family size have received the government aid while the percentage of government aid in large family size is nil.

Therefore, in general, the findings suggest that the women of small family size are more backward and that is why they aspire for job, they receive financial aid and they face greater Hardship.

The results regarding level of education (Table 20) indicated that there was hundred per cent illiteracy in the respondent's own education, the illiteracy rate of father's education was 93%. The percentage of matriculate father was only 7%. In the adult education dimension the figure were most promising as all the women (N=240) were receiving adult education.

Following observations were made in the level of education :

(a) The respondent's own education and father's education the percentage of small family size was almost equal (84.16 and 85.11). The results also showed that even in the high illiteracy group the percentage of large family size was only 7.50% and 14.89%. It was also outstanding to note that in case of matriculate fathers the percentage of small family was 56.97 while the percentage of large family size was only 3.03.

The findings suggest that the women with little or no education have developed awareness about the family planning and therefore, the majority of illiterate women have a small family size. It is a very good start and it will help the women to curb their socio-economic backwardness.

TABLE 20

Education and Other Relevant Variables : Percentage Only

Name of the variables / Education		Family members		Income		Nature and type of Expenditure			Service orientation		Government Aid
		0-9	10 or above	Below 500	Above 500	Joint Expd.	Self-dependent	Hardship dependent	Desire for service	Choice for service	
Own Education N = 240	1. 100%	84.16	7.50	41.66	22.50	80.00	23.75	35.41	50.00	43.33	5.41
Father's Education	1. N = 215	85.11	14.89	51.16	9.76	80.93	23.72	39.06	45.11	57.67	4.65
	2. N = 25	56.97	3.03	64	36%	68.00	24.00	48.00	44.00	44.009	12%
	3. 100%										
Adult Education N = 22	2 22	73.87	7.65	37.83	17.56	70.72	22.52	39.63	45.05	39.18	5.85

Note : 1. Indicates Illiterate
2. Indicate above matric
3. Indicate above graduate
The different N are given for each category

So, even in the poor women the conception of large family size is losing its salience which is the need of the hour.

(b) The result of *Income* variable (Table 21) indicates that 41.66 illiterate women were in low income group. The percentage of low income group women was slightly higher in illiterate and matriculate fathers (51.16 per cent and 64 per cent).

The percentage of women in high income group was 22.80, 9.76 and 36 per cent respectively. Even the percentage of income group women in adult education was only 17.86 while it was more than double (37.83) for low income group.

The findings suggest that the majority of women are in low income group and the percentage of high income group women are not at all fascinating. Since the monthly income of an individual has been considered as one the most objective indicators of one's financial condition, therefore. the present result provides solid ground for the financial backwardness among the women.

(c) The nature and type of expenditure is also an important indicator of the economic backwardness. This variable yielded the following results :

   (i) The 80% illiterate women and 80% illiterate fathers spend their income *jointly*. The percentage of joint expenditure in matriculate fathers was 68.00 and 70.72 per cent women of adult education programme were spending the income jointly.

   (ii) The percentage of self-dependent women was only 23.75 is illiterate women group and 23.92 is illiterate father's group. The percentage was almost similar (24.1) for matriculate fathers.

   (iii) Only 35.41 to 48.00 per cent women reported about their financial hardship. So, the percentage of hardship was below average.

The above finding again substantiates the investigators earlier contention that due to the over emphasis on

TABLE 21
Income and Other Relevant Variables : Percentage Only

Income	Nature and type of expenditure			Service Orientation		Government Aid
	Joint Expd.	Self-Dependent	Hardship	Desire for service	Choice for service	
Below 500 N=99	67.67	27.27	72.72	38.38	52.32	3.03
500 or above N=44	15.90	11.36	45.45	56.81	42.11	22.72

joint expenditure the women do not face hardship monetary problems.

(*d*) The results of *desire for service* and *choice of service* in rural/urban places that only 50% or below 50% women had expressed their desire for service. The occupational mobility was slightly higher in the illiterate fathers group *i.e.*, 57.67.

(*e*) Except in the case of matriculate fathers, the percentage of government aid was almost similar in each group *i.e.*, illiterate women, illiterate fathers and adult education. The relative percentage were 5.41, 5.85 and 4.65. The percentage of government aid provided to the income of matriculate fathers was 12%.

It seems that due to high education the matriculate fathers have succeeded in receiving loans or financial aid from the government.

The above table showed that out of 240 women only 143 women endorsed their monthly income. Out of 143, 44 women were in high income group while rest 99 were in low income group.

The income table yielded the following results regarding the other indicators of economical status of women.

(*f*) In low income group 67.67 per cent women adhere to the principle of joint expenditure and a large percentage reported about the hardship. The percentage of economically *self-dependent* was also high in low income group. Whereas, in high income group only 15.96 per cent women have reported the joint expenditure but 45.45 per cent women were in financial crisis and only 11.36 women were self-dependent. However, the percentage of economically self-dependent was higher in low income group *i.e.*, 27.27.

The findings, further supplement the nation of high economic backwardness among the women of low income group.

The most interesting result was obtained in the case of *service orientation* because the women of high income group were more keen for their service, and the percentage of desire for service in low income group was only 38.38.

The findings indirectly explains the lack of motivation in the women of low income group.

(g) So for the government aid is concerned it was ridiculous to note that the larger percentage of women belonging to high income group received more government aid than the women of low income group.

The last Table 22 of this chapter reveals that there were 114 women in *joint expenditure*—77 women in *hardship* category and only 32 were *self-dependent*.

(a) Table 22 shows that the joint expenditure and occupational mobility were endorsed highly by the women of both categories, *i.e.*, (i) Women who believed in joint expenditure and (ii) Women who were self-dependent. The relative percentage were 98.29 and 96.87 for desire for service and 78.98 and 78.1 for occupational mobility. The women of Hardship category have endorsed the dimensions very low. Hence the result is not in the expected direction. Because it is assumed that women of Hardship category would have a strong *service orientation*.

(b) It is remarkable to note that the higher percentage of *hardship womem* received the government aid, *i.e.*, 11.68 while 7.89 per cent women of *joint expenditure* received the government aid and the percentage was further low (3.12) in the women of economically *self-dependent* category.

The result of nature and type of expenditure revealed that the women who are financially more backward and who face economical problems do not aspire either for service or for choice of service.

It reveals a negative aspect of the women because the lack of service orientation in women will hamper their further growth.

At the same time it has been found that the larger percentage of women in the hardship category have received financial aid from the government and that is why they do not aspire for the service.

Summing up one can generalize that the findings of most of the indicators are in support of the investigators' assumption that there is greater socio-economic backwardness in the women of lower strata.

Table 22
Nature and Type of Expenditure and Other Relevant Variables : Percentage Only

Name of the variables Nature and type of Expenditure	Service Orientation		Government Aid
	Desire for service	Choice for service	
Joint Expenditure N=114	98.24	78.95	7.89
Self Dependent N=32	96.87	78.12	3.12
Hardship N=77	45.45	31.16	11.68

CHAPTER IV

SUMMARY AND CONCLUSIONS

Since the socio-economic status of an individual is an overlapping term, it is very difficult to segregate the two, 'Social' and 'Economic', as the separate entities. Hence it is assumed that the social position of an individual will be determined by his economic condition and *vice versa*. However, the intensity of socio-economic needs varies in the different sections of the society. The problem of economic condition is more severe in the lower class people while in 'middle class' and 'upper class' the problem of social status is more acute.

Therefore, in the present study, an attempt has been made to identify the relevant indicators of socio-economic backwardness, with the major focus on the women of lower class. So the present study was undertaken with a view to conduct a survey of the women of Bhagalpur town.

1. Method

The sample included the 240 women of proper Bhagalpur with an age range between 15 to 35. For the present purpose only those women were selected who come under the adult education programme.

A structured interview schedule was prepared. The schedule consisted of items regarding the different indicator of socio-economic status, for example, caste, background, marital status, income, nature and type of expenditure, level of education etc. These indicators were grouped into four broad categories *i.e.*, (*a*) Social (*b*) Educational (*c*) Economic and (*d*) Others. Most of the indicators had its sub-categories too.

The data were collected in the class-room situation of adult education centres. As much as 240 schedules were returned and found suitable for further analysis.

2. Main Findings of the Study

The findings of the present study were divided into two sections, *Section I* and *Section II.*

Here the results of the present study will be presented under different categories. Each category will include the findings regarding the different indicators of socio-economic backwardness of women of lower class.

Social Indicators

The main findings of this area are as follows :

(a) The majority of the low caste women belonged to the backward caste while only 21 per cent women belonged to forward caste.

(b) The social status of lower class women is not affected by their marital status as most of the women were married (66.66 per cent), almost half of them were unmarried and a low percentage was widow (2.92 per cent).

(c) The pattern of living suggested that in India the collectivist orientation is gradually losing its weight as half of the population live with their husband in nuclear family.

(d) Even in lower class women the larger family size is not encouraged.

(e) Occupation-wise 86.33 per cent women were engaged in business while only 11.67 per cent women were in service.

The results of the social indicators suggest that the social status of lower class women is not at the grassroot level rather their social status is passing through the phase of transition where neither they are socially more backward nor they are fully advance. Some of the indicators like preference for small family size, individualistic orientation and their marital condition etc. Support their enhancement.

The other side of the coin suggests that by caste and by

occupation they are still backward but still their over all social backwardness is not intense. This is mainly due to the fact that women of the present study are urban women who are invariably influenced by the modern technological changes.

So due to urbanization the women of lower class have succeeded in improving their social status. So far their backwardness in caste is concerned, the government has made special arrangement for their admission, examinations and appointments. Therefore, we hope that the reservation policy of government will help the backward caste to go up in the social ladder.

Educational Indicators

(a) The figure of the level of education, particularly in case of respondents own education was most depressive, at all the women (N = 240) were found to be illiterate.

(b) In case of father's education the 89.55% fathers were illiterate while 10 per cent were above matric and only one father was a graduate.

(c) The adult education programme is most successful here because all the women were receiving the adult education.

(d) But none of them have reported about their specific training.

The women of lower class have presented a very poor picture of their educational status as the illiteracy rate is hundred per cent. Not only the respendents but respondent's father's educational level was also very poor as 89.55% fathers were illiterate.

The educational backwardness among the women may be attributed to the fact that in Indian society there is over emphasis on the gender role *i.e.*, a female should be submissive, dutiful and homely. Therefore, it is correct to state that in India the social attitudes to girl's education vary from acceptable to the level of indifference. Even today the people do not understand that 'education is a universal right not is class privilege' (S. Radhakrishnan). If education is a human right the daughter in any community should be given colateral opportunity for access to education. But the data showed that in practice it is far from what it should be. Even a cursory glance on the uneven development of education as between the sexes establishes the fact (Nandi, 1984).

Now it seems reasonable to conclude that due to the several reasons the lower class women are educationally more backward than their counterpart.

However, to raise the educational standard the government has started many adult education centres especially for women. Similarly government decision about free education up to class VII, free distribution of books and lunch packets are the major steps through which high class illiteracy rate can be removed.

So we hope that in near future the educational backwardness of the lower women will be minimized.

Economic Indicators

The specific results obtained on the basis of economic indicators are given below :

(a) The majority of women are below poverty line as out of 240 women the 175 were earning an income below Rs. 500 while only 27.08% women were in 500 group.

(b) Nature and type of expenditure revealed that 81.11 per cent women believe in joint expenditure. Almost 50 per cent were facing the financial crisis and only one fourth women were economically self-dependent.

(c) In service orientation only 50 per cent women were keen to to seek the job and almost the same percentage were ready move to either rural or urban areas for their job.

(d) The data indicated a very poor performance of the government in providing financial aid to the low class women as only 5 per cent women received the government aid.

The results suggest that there is absolute economic backwardness in the women of lower class. Because majority of them are below poverty line and fifty per cent of them face regular financial crisis. At the same time the percentage for the desire of service and occupational mobility is only 50% while only 5% of them received the government aid.

All these indicate the poor economical condition of the women This is due to the fact that in Indian society the economic independence among women was less emphasized. Traditionally, women were not allowed to go outside (the four walls) of their home for job. Though there are a number of employed women but most of these women belong to middle class or upper class. So the employment among women is a very recent phenomena. So far the employment among lower class women is concerned, first of all lower class women get seasonal employment and even if they are employed they are paid lower wages and due to the family pressure their drop out rate is very high. The failure of government in providing loans or financial aid to the poor women is also one of the major causes of their economic backwardness.

Verma (1984) has observed that due to generation gap the young girls of the society are seeking more employment to raise their economic status. Because the employed or working women have more 'a say' in their family and they are looked upon as 'something' and not as 'nothing'.

So, to raise the women's economic status, it is necessary that women should exert more and more for employment so that they may add some income to the family.

Other Indicators

This indicator includes the result about the nature and type of activities in which the lower class women are engaged. The majority of women have reported that they are engaged in household activities, some have reported about other work and a few percentage are engaged in the knitting and sewing work.

The greater involvement of women with the household affairs suggests that the role of housewife is more important for women. They do not think anything beyond this and even if they are employed or highly educated it is their duty to manage the house. Although this role is not at all paying, they do not receive any return except some regards from their children or husbands minus, it is high time that the role of housewife must be abolished and the gender role must be abolished.

If the role of housewife still continues then their must be

some fixed wages for this role too (Prasad, 1984), so that they may have a feeling of achievement and they will get an earned recognition. Because unearned recognition is not a substitute for an earned recognition.

Secondly housewife should learn the techniques of time saving so that they may utilize their energy in knitting, tailoring, nursing etc.

Therefore, only the household activities are not enough to raise the overall status of women rather women should minimize their charm and attraction towards the home and the family and they should come forward.

3. Supplementary Findings of the Study

Apart from the main findings, there are some supplementary findings too. It is hoped that these findings will be helpful in providing a logical base for the future research.

Some of the notable findings of the study are as follows :

(a) There is hundred per cent illiteracy in the women of lower strata.

(b) The level of education is slightly better in forward caste group.

(c) Majority of them are below poverty line. The figure of high income group (Rs. 500 or above) is not at all fescinating.

(d) There is a general lack of motivation among the women for service orientation.

(e) The family size is independent of the caste group, women irrespective of their caste and class prefer to have small family.

(f) The women of small family size are more pragmatic as they have greater desire for service.

(g) The women of small family size receive more financial aid and they face greater hardship.

(h) The service class women possess better educational background as in this class some matriculate and graduate fathers are located.

(i) The two classes (service and business) did not differ in their service orientation.

(*j*) The high percentage of business class women received more government aid.

(*k*) Due to joint expenditure the low percentage of women face monetary hardship.

(*l*) Even today the women are more collectivists as they cling to their ingroup and spend their income jointly.

(*m*) The matriculate fathers have succeeded most in receiving financial aid for the government.

(*n*) The women reporting greater economical hardship received more financial aid.

4. The Socio-Economic Condition of Women—An Evaluation

It has been observed that the socio-economic condition of women belonging to the lower strata is more miserable. This is partly due to the social system and partly the women are themselves responsible for their disgraceful positions in the society.

So far the society is concerned the Indian society is primarily a male dominated society where little or no change is expected. If in any case the change is being introduced then one has to face multiple problems. In most cases, it is the women who resents to these changes and who shows her inability to adjust to these changes. Therefore, it seems that the women are more 'socially bounded' to their old values and they are not at all aware with their existence in the society. The lack of clarity in women about their 'status', 'exploitation' and economic deprivation'. That is, even if a wife is severely beaten by her husband she never complains or she seldom goes to the police station for lodging F.I.R. Similarly, if a husband brings a second wife, the first wife does not leave her home or husband rather she has to adjust to this new situation, because in India the husbands are treated as equal to God. More often, an earning wife has to face economic deprivation because she has to surrender her total income to her husband and she has no right to spend even a single pie out of her own salary.

So, these are some of the behavioural indicators which explain that why the women of lower strata are more backward than the women of any other sections of the society.

Here the investigator feels that it would not be an exaggeration if we accept that women are not only the 'losers' rather they are 'misfits' for the society.

The discussion ultimately leads one to some socio-economic problems of women belonging to the lower strata. The problems which need more attention from the government and from the societies are as follows :

(a) By caste and class women of lower strata are more backward

(b) Business is their main occupation

(c) The low level of education

(d) Lack of training and skill

(e) Majority of them are below poverty line

(f) Lower percentage of economic self dependence

(g) Low motivation for desire of Service and occupational mobility

(h) Absence of government aid

(i) The unrewarding household activities

(j) Poor conception of time

The socio-economic problems of the women of lower strata are more or less structured therefore, it, is easy to specify the measures for its solution. Though one cannot give assurance for its total elimination but one can minimize its severity.

Some Measures to Solve Their Problems

It has been widely accepted that the radical steps have been taken by the government to reduce the intensity of the problems. These measures include the reservation policy by which nearly 30 to 50 per cent seats are reserved for the backward castes. Similarly opening of various training centres with the provision of stipend, providing financial aid to start new business and streamlining the adult education programme are some of the positive efforts in this direction.

Yet it has been found that the various schemes of government have not proved effective. In some cases, the government itself is not very consistent and clear about its policies, while in others the *via media* or the agencies are not very cooperative *i.e.*, these agencies do not understand the urgency of the problems and therefore, they fail to serve its purpose, so we have to look for some viable alternatives which can help the poor women in solving their socio-economic problems. In this context, the services rendered by the voluntary organizations are more important because it is the only organization which can render such public services. Now-a-days they also assist them in solving their problems. The best of it is that it does not discriminate women on the basis of their caste and class, educational level, rural-urban background, etc. rather it extends help to the women of all categories.

The impact of voluntary organizations would be more fruitful if they also take into consideration that whether 'legal' and 'functional' literacy are provided to these women. If 'yes' what should be the syllabi. The courses must include the topic like child marriage property rights, wage acts, family planning, child care, nutrition and hygiene.

Similarly this organization should also look into that way the different government schemes fail to achieve its targets. Where are the loopholes? Why the poor women do not receive even minimum education? For which an evaluation of the adult education programme should be started just to improve its function.

So far the government aid is concerned the role of different agencies should be carefully re-examined and they should be instructed to avoid 'red tapism' and 'beaurocracy' in granting the loans etc.

At the same time the household activities of women should get full recognition and should be paid minimum wages for it the women should also learn the techniques of time savings, that is structuring of time and structuring of daily routine, so that they may utilize their time in part time job, or some other paid work like tailoring, knitting, nursing, etc.

But nothing can be achieved until there is general awareness in the common people that they should work for a common cause *i.e.*, the uplifting the condition of women belonging to lower socio-economic strata.

BIBLIOGRAPHY

Chandrakala, A. Hate (1969), *Changing Status of Women*, Allied Publishers, Bombay.

Gulati, Saroj (1985), *Women and Society, Northern India in 11th and 12th Centuries*, Chanakya Publications, New Delhi, p. 256

Jones, A.C. (1980), *Observation the Current Status of Women in India*, International Journal of Women's Studies 3 (1), pp. 1-118.

Manohar, M.K. (1980), *Socio-Economic Status of Indian Women*, Seema Publications, New-Delhi, pp. 1-30

Mohsini, S.R. (1973), *Adult Education and Community Education : An Indian Experiment*, Indian Adult Education Association, New Delhi, p. 26

Nandi, Ramola (1984), *The Paradox of Inequality*, Legal Status of Women in India, Volume edited by S.M. College, Bhagalpur, pp. 29-35.

Prasad, R. (1984), *Economic Status of Women in India*, Legal Status of Women in India, Vol. Edt. by S.M. College, Bhagalpur, pp. 12-16.

Rao, N.J. Usha (1983), *Women in a Developing Society*, Ashish Publishing House, New Delhi.

Singh, S. (1957), *History of Adult Education During British Period*, Indian Adult Education Association, Delhi.

Talwar, Usha (1964), *Social Profile of Working Women*, Varshaney Printing Press, Delhi,

Vedalankar, Sharda (1984), *The Social Status of Women in Bihar*, Legal Status of Women in India, Vol. Edt. by S.M. College, Bhagalpur, pp. 17-28.

Verma, Neelam (1984), *Generation Gap and Changes in Status of Women*, Legal Status of Women in India, Vol. Edt. by S.M. College, Bhagalpur, pp. 204-12

Wali Azra (1984), *The Status of Women in a Man's World in Different Economic Strata*, Legal Status of Women in India, Vol. Edt. by S.M. College, Bhagalpur, pp. 175-82

INDEX